POETRY by SIMON

VOLUME 2: CIRCLE OF LIFE – THE VERSHELLE CATO EXPERIENCE

ROY LEE "SIMON" JARMON

Poetry By Simon

Volume 2: Circle of Life —
The VERSHELLE CATO Experience

Roy Lee "Simon" Jarmon

ISBN: 978-1-967375-50-9 (Paperback)

ISBN: 978-1-967375-51-6 (E-book)

Library of Congress Control Number: 2025914740

Printed in the United States of America

Published by:

QUIPPY™
QUILL

info@thequippyquill.com
(302) 295-2278

Table of Contents

MILITARY INSPIRATIONS - HEALING WOUNDS

LOVE, ROMANCE AND SUCH

IN MEMORY OF

Nathalyn Vershelle Cato Jarmon, my late wife, without whom I would have never realized what GOD meant in the scriptures when HE said that "two shall become one" as well as the phrase "…'til Death we do part." She was a compassionate Christian woman of True Faith in her GOD and projected HIS Loving Spirit everywhere she went and toward everyone she met. She was a Master Teacher. She could teach anyone – through encouragement and dedication – to do anything that she would ask. She was truly one of GOD's angels. I shall always remember her musical talent, whereby she could make that church's organ talk to you like a natural person. And I will never forget that wonderful and heartfelt laugh of hers. Rest in Peace in God's bosom, Vershelle. Because of you, I now view people and the world in a different, more Godly way.

PREFACE

I want to send my heartfelt thanks to the members and heads of the following organizations:

Ebenezer Baptist Church in New Brunswick, NJ, **Traveler's Baptist Church in Piscataway, NJ, First Baptist Church** in Bound Brook, NJ, **St. Albans Church** on Lee Avenue in New Brunswick, NJ, **Sharon Baptist** in New Brunswick, NJ, **Somerset Presbyterian Church** in Somerset, NJ, and **St. Matthew Baptist Church** in Roselle, NJ.

Also, **The Sisters' Network of Central New Jersey Inc, The Deacons Alliance of Central New Jersey**, and The **Tiny Tots Spot** in New Brunswick, NJ.

A great shout-out of Kudos to **Loretha Payne, Linda Wilson, Shirlene Phillips, Mrs. Ira Dais, Ernestine Jones, Angela Hill Laster,** and **Barbara Jenkins.**

And a special thanks to **Carl Jones** and **Emma Johnson** for their editing.

Roy Lee 'Simon' Jarmon
Author

DISCLAIMER

These writings are expressions formulated from my thoughts, opinions, and fantasies that I have acquired during my lifetime. I have used many names in my writings; however, these names do not reflect the true identity of any particular person or individual, unless specifically stated. The names used by me are for rhythmic, iambic and/or poetic reasons only and do not apply to any particular or specific person, place or thing.

Spouse, Friends
and
Dedications

HOW LONG (MAYBE NOT UNTIL I AM COMPLETE)

(Written to my late wife Nathalyn Vershelle Cato Sanders
before we were married, in hope to win her heart and make her my wife.
This is an extension to a previous poem.)

The water roars thunderously
    As it splashes powerfully
    Upon huge boulders
    With gigantic strength.

The boulders will stand, unmovable –
    As if at attention –
    While the liquid burden
    Soaks his steady shoulders.

We all know that, for time unknown,
    The rock will stand
    With great resistance.

We also know that the stone
    Will grow smaller and smaller
    As the water falls with
    Constant power until the
    Boulder melts to a pebble –
    And beyond.

She is the water and I
    Am the boulder.
How long will I stand?
How long will it be
    Before I am dissolved?

How long will it be before
    I become a planted pebble?
How long before I am planted
    To blossom into some beautiful thing?

Maybe, not until I am complete:
With love constantly in the air.
With trust abounding everywhere.

Maybe, not until I am complete.
With arms outstretched and open wide.
With a family that doesn't have to swallow its pride.
With 'I LOVE YOU', a daily prayer.
With a heart of gold always there.

Maybe, not until I am complete.
But when it's all said and tried and true,
    I can never be complete
    When I am not with you,
    Because I love you Nathalyn Vershelle.

Roy Lee 'Simon' Jarmon

NEEDS

(Written to /for/ and about my late wife Nathalyn Vershelle Cato
before we were married)

The fish swims adroitly in the sea:
    Sometimes weaving, sometimes floating.
The brilliant sparks of light
    Glitters from its scales
    And creates a colorful joyfulness.
Remove the fish from the water
    And it flops helplessly
    And then quickly dies.
The fish needs the sea.

The flowers spring upward through
    The hard-packed earth and
    Spryly smiles as the gentle rain
    Drenches the earth and its arms;
    Swaying happily with the raindrops
    Diving from its petals and
    Running down its stems.
Remove the flower from the earth
    And it soon withers and dies.
The flowers need the earth and the rain.

The body is a very complicated machine
    With muscles, tendons, bones, and blood
    That unites to work many wonders
    And perform miraculous feats of strength.
Without oxygen in the blood and
    Food to nourish the muscles and bones
    The body soon becomes cold, stiff, lifeless clay.

The body needs food and oxygen.
My heart shouts with happiness and
>   Joy when showered with love and affection.
To remove that love from me
>   Would cause my heart to break
>   Into a million – if not more – pieces and
>   (I'm sure)
>   I would soon become non-existent
My heart and I need that love and affection, and
>   No one can give that love like you
My heart and I need you
>   heart and I need Vershelle.

Roy Lee 'Simon' Jarmon

I'M LOVE

(Written to my late wife – Nathalyn Vershelle Cato Jarmon)

That LOVE is a beautiful feeling is true.
I've found it after searching my whole life through.

LOVE is the answer if you need a heart mender.
LOVE is for real. It's not a pretender.

LOVE is the key to every dreamer's stride,
For LOVE is surely wider than wide.

LOVE is such a beautiful feeling.
For any topless heart, it becomes a ceiling.

LOVE changes the color of any shade of blue.
It's the answer for people like me and you.

LOVE takes the lonesomeness from any dreary place;
And any old scar it can easily erase.

Anytime you're sad and really feeling down,
LOVE puts a smile over any old frown.

When your life's just a big mountain to scale,
LOVE makes a heaven of this earthly hell.

When you get to a wall that you can't go around,
You can depend on LOVE. It won't let you down.

So, when you're lonely and LOVE's well overdue,
You can depend on me, Darling. I'm LOVE for you.

Roy Lee "Simon" Jarmon (goppy)

TO VERSHELLE: IN APPRECIATION
(NO "ME" WITHOUT "YOU")

*(Written to and read to my then wife Nathalyn Vershelle Cato Jarmon
at one of our marriage enhancement meetings)*

I believe that I am a true proponent of the poem that someone
wrote, which says,
"Once a task has begun,
Never leave it until it's done.
Be that task large or small,
Do it well or not at all."

This is not to say that I can, or even do, a better job than anyone
else does. But it is a feeble attempt to show why I am usually found on
one extreme tangent of the pendulum or the other. I seem to need to
'see' things in a logical fashion, where something starts and then it ends,
even if it's a step, a phase, or a procedure in some overall continuum. In
that sense, it has meaning and purpose, showing the essence of
completeness.

Vershelle, you know how I like things to be orderly or in a step-by-
step fashion. You know that I like the top put back on the toothpaste or
the cap back on the bottle. Or how I say 'this' should follow 'that' in a
chronological order. Well, that's what keeps me stable, because when
things are in order, I can better foresee whether these things are
completeness or not. Without completeness (or some resemblance), I
just can't function.

There's no soothing comfort like the warmth and softness of your
body pressed firmly against mine. There's no passion or ecstatic joy that
I could have envisioned compared to the way you make me feel when
we make love. There is no way to express the gaiety and delight that
your gift of laughter performs as it captures my heart and fills the walls
of our home. These things I like! These things I want! And these things

I need and get – from you! And, as important and crucial as they are, they only scratch the surface of what you really mean to me.

It may sound as if I'm saying more about myself than about you. However, until you understand me – my inferiorities, my iniquities, and my inabilities – you cannot begin to fathom how important you are to me. So I shall give a few examples.

First, take the baseball player who steps up to the plate and hits the ball out of the park! Over the wall! Everyone yells, "Home run!" but no score is granted or recorded until he goes around and touches first base, second base, third base, and then home plate. Only then is the home run complete. Every step, every phase must be completed. Whatever I do, you are the one who ensures that all my bases are touched. You make my accomplishments complete.

Next, take an airplane! That's a huge machine that has many parts. To attach each part together with the utmost security and with the least wind resistance, one uses rivets. For some small things like sneakers, weight-lifting belts, and the like that needs to be fastened quickly, one uses Velcro. A house, with all of its corners and angles, would crumble and come crashing down if someone began removing the many nails that holds it together, and when your delicate and precious ornaments topple and break, glue – used with patience and caring – can make them whole again. You are the rivets of my life, the Velcro of my sanity, the nails of my world, and the glue of my heart.

And, not only that, my love! I – alone – am incomplete. There are holes. There are snags. There are missing pieces. And where these imperfections reside in me, you fill the gaps and the voids. Where there is space, you fit in like a cogwheel. Now, I can rotate and work and be of some use, but only because of you. Yes! I must face the fact that there is no "<u>ME</u>" without "<u>YOU</u>".

But now looms two big questions. The first question is, "How did I exist before you came into my life?" However, the more important question is, "Now, that you have become a part of my life, could I ever exist without you?" In answering that question, I am inclined to shout an emphatic, "No!" No! No, I must face the fact that there is no "<u>ME</u>" without "<u>YOU</u>".

Without the sun, most life would wilt and decay. But, with too much sun and no rain, things would become parched, dry up, and die. You are the sunshine and the rain in my life – in the right portions. You are my weakness where I'm strong and my strength where I'm weak. Yes, we fit together like cogwheels. We belong together like the hand and glove. No! No! I must face the fact that there is no "<u>ME</u>" without "<u>YOU</u>".

Now that I have said all of that, I would like to tell you how much I love you. I would like to tell you how much I love you, but I can't. I can't because I have so much of it that I haven't been able to measure it all. And not only that, my Dear, it's still growing.

So I'll conclude by saying, "Vershelle, I love you now and I <u>always</u> <u>will</u> with <u>all</u> my heart."

Roy Lee "Simon" Jarmon (goppy)

MY DREAM

Sometimes I'm here all alone,
But I'm not lonely because
I'm filled with thoughts of you.
You are in my mind,
    In my heart,
And as I think of you –
    I dream of you.
Really, I dream of US.

I dream that when I awaken,
My first movement is not
    To stretch, not
    To yarn, but
    To reach for you!
To feel you there –
    Lying there –
    Beside me in my bed.

To know that the Woman
Who took the day's work?
    The day's toil,
    and the day's strenuous activity
out of my bones,
    my muscles, and
    my body

To know that you are a Friend
Who erased from my mind
The discriminating facets of life
And the relentless viciousness
Out of my bones.

To know that you are the Lover
Who so gently lowers my strength
In such a passionate –
Yet compassionate –
    Endeavor.

To know that you are the Wife
Who knows and shares
    My thoughts,
    My faults,
    My feelings
In such an unyielding fashion.

Oh, yes, I reach for you.
In a simultaneous movement of my
Blinking eyes when I first awake –
I reach for you.

And, as I thank God for
A brand-new day,
I thank Him for you –
    For you and your Love.

Roy Lee 'Simon' Jarmon

MY FIRST OFFICIAL BALD HEAD

Where I grew up, a bald head was frowned upon. It was not considered a death sentence, but it certainly wasn't fashionable. And they were always – for the most part – old or elderly men. "There goes bald-headed Mr. Frank" or "Oh, you talking about old slick head Curtis?" or "I don't see what she sees in that no-haired Tommy Lee" are the type of phrases that I always heard.

That's what all the older women were saying. Well, they were older than men because I was just a little kid. I may not have always known what they meant, but I knew what they said. I knew what I heard. See, I was like a cat. You know how that small kitten is always purring and rubbing itself around your ankles? Those little kittens wrap themselves around your ankles like Velcro.

You move your leg, and it's still there. You can lift your leg, and it's still there – hanging on. You can try and walk away, but it's still there. Hanging around. That was me. I would be snuggled or nestled next to whichever lady was willing on that day. Or I may be sitting quietly in a corner – just out of the light or out of their peripheral vision. Or I would sometimes sit on the porch swinging my legs and reading – or pretending to read – my A-B-C book.

Oh, yes! I heard a lot of talk from the women. They would talk very freely because they knew that I probably didn't always understand what they meant. But I know what they said, and I know what I heard. And they were partial to bald-headed people. "Ain't no way I'd take that from old bald-headed Billy Joe!" one of them said.

Yes, bald heads were somewhat frowned upon. I was crushed and speechless, and my heart ached fiercely when I first saw it. I had brought her breakfast-in-bed. As I positioned myself between the wall and the left side of the bed, I placed the tray of bacon and eggs, and toast on the lamp stand. "I hope I didn't overcook the eggs," I said as I placed the palm of my left hand in the middle of her back and raised her to a sitting position.

That's when I noticed it. Laying there on her pillow, a huge clump of her hair. I was inclined to hurriedly snatch the clump and hide it somewhere so that she wouldn't see it, but I felt that a quick movement like that would bring her attention to it.

That's when it all came gushing out and slapped a crushing blow to my heart and soul. It was as if someone was pouring it from a bucket onto my head. It covered me so quickly and thoroughly that I became weak in my knees. For a moment, I could not breathe. When I did finally catch my breath, I realized that there were tears in my eyes. There were tears from mixed emotions. I hated to hear her in that situation, but the words that kept ringing in my ears and soul gave me a renewed sense of hope.

I knew that I couldn't deceive her in this predicament because she/we needed to handle it as God prescribed. The words kept erupting from my soul. "You shall know the TRUTH and the TRUTH shall make you FREE!!!"

That's when I showed it to her. I slowly reached my balled fist toward her and gradually began uncurling my fingers one by one. She looked at the clump of hair in my hand. And, to my surprise, she smiled and said in her weak, slow, and nearly hoarse voice, "My hair. They said that it would be falling out. Chemo- does that to people, you know?" I was shocked to hear her say that in such a calm and matter-of-fact way, especially given the way that I know she felt about her hair. She loved to have her hair neat and beautiful, whether wig or not.

I was so relieved to hear her tone until I looked into her eyes. Those big, bright eyes of hers that had lit up so many rooms and healed so many broken (and seemingly doomed) hearts looked dim and cold. That wasn't her. I now realize that her bold and brave statement about her hair was to spare me. Now, that's her! Always thinking about the other person. She was definitely God's angel in that way. Even during her time of trials and agony, she was considering others and not herself.

I got her breakfast tray settled and hurried out into the other room. I could not allow her to see me cry. I ran into the living room and knelt affront the loveseat and cried and prayed. No, I couldn't let her see me crying. Seeing others in pain would be the worst thing that I could do to her.

The cry and prayer did me good. It calmed me somewhat. It released a lot of bottled tension that had been festering within me for some time now. Ever since the cancer – that dreaded, ugly, deadly, monstrous and frightful disease – was discovered, I had been baffled and confused. Someone who didn't smoke and didn't drink has contracted this horrific and horrendous disease. Someone who had such a healthy body and ate in such a healthy way has contracted this uncalled-for ailment. Someone who loved the Lord (God) and considered others ('...love thy neighbor as thyself...') had contracted this God-forsaken affliction.

Yes, it was time for a little relief. Just think! She's lying there saturated with these deadly cells, and I'm the one feeling sad! Feeling sorrowful! But it's time that I returned and put away her tray. I'm sure that she has finished eating by now. She hasn't been eating much anyway since she started the chemotherapy. She said that everything tastes like metal. Nonetheless, I had better go and get the plate.

To my surprise, she had eaten more than I had expected. She was sitting up and playing with her hair. "I see you ate a little food this time," I said, putting up a strong front to smile.

"Yes. It was good! I lost my appetite when I started thinking about my hair," she said in a voice that sounded much more positive than I had anticipated. Her voice was strong, but her hair was a mess. Every time she rubbed her hand through her hair, some would break off into her hand. I hate to say it this way, but her hair looked stringy, brittle, and kinky.

I kissed her forehead, took the plate and tray, and left the room. I returned shortly with my hair clippers. I didn't say a word. I stood at the foot of the bed and held the clippers up in the air. She knew what I meant. She smiled. A big smile, too. "Do I have enough hair to cut?" she asked.

"There are some patches that have quite a bit of hair," I said. "Maybe I'll just even it out, okay?"

"No! Just cut it all off."

"Are you sure?" I asked, surprised at her answer.

"Sure!" she said.

It didn't take long to cut it off because her hair was so thin and brittle. And, too, there were just a few patches left. I finished and rubbed her smooth head as we both smiled while staring deeply and lovingly into each other's eyes.

I went into the bathroom to put the clippers away. That's when it hit me. She loves her hair, and yet she was willing to cut it all off. The least that I can do is cut my hair so that we'll both have the same haircut. Yes, that's what I'll do! That'll show my support.

Just as I was finishing up with my bald trim, our son came running into the bathroom from playing outside. "Dad!" he said, stunned. "Why are you cutting your hair like that? You look bald!"

"It's to support Mom. You know that her medicine made her hair fall out. So, I'm cutting my head bald for support," I said.

"Can I get a bald head too?" he asked, to my surprise.

"Are you sure, son?"

"Yes, Dad!"

"Okay, then" I said, feeling proud of his willingness to offer support to the family.

Our son and I walked into the bedroom and stood at the foot of the bed, a wry smile on our lips. She was lying motionless with her eyes closed. Realizing that we were there, she gradually opened her eyes. We all looked at each other for a while, and then we burst into laughter. We laughed out loud and heartily. And as we wiped the tears of laughter from our eyes, she exclaimed, "We are the bald-head family!" And the roar of laughter again filled the room, dissolving the gloom of this dreaded affliction – a moment of respite well desired and very well deserved.

Yes, that was my first and official bald head. May you never have to experience that choice under those circumstances.

Roy Lee 'Simon' Jarmon

TALK TO ME

"Good morning, my Dear! How are you feeling on this lovely, sun-shining morning? We just went through another rough night, didn't we? I think that was the roughest night that we've ever had – so far – don't you? Well, I'm glad to see that you – we – made it through the night. There seems to be a little smile on your lips this morning. One thing is for sure: it's time. It's time that you smiled for a change. It's time that you have a restful night, too. At least once in a while, you should be able to have a restful night's sleep. Yes, that would be nice, wouldn't it? To have a restful night's sleep every now and then? Would be nice, wouldn't it? I'm sure you would like that. I know that I would! I hate to see you feeling restless all the time. Tossing and turning all night! Grimacing and groaning all night! That's not good. Yes! Yes, you do. You deserve to have a restful night's sleep sometimes."

"What do you want to eat for breakfast this morning? Have you thought about it? What would you like me to fix for you? What about some eggs? Baby, talk to me. There's cereal. There's cold cereal and milk. Or would you prefer hot cereal? Maybe oatmeal or grits? Talk to me, Babe."

"Maybe you'd like to start with a small glass of juice or milk, huh? Or maybe coffee, or tea, or hot chocolate, Dear? What about some toast? We have cinnamon and raisin toast, my Love! I know that you love that! Come on, Sweetheart, talk to me. Why are you not talking to me?"

"All right, then. I'll cook whatever I feel like cooking. You know you have to eat something before you take your medicine. And you know what? We have to change your pain patch today, also. Make sure that you remind me so that I don't forget, okay? You're very quiet this morning! Come on, Babe! Talk to me!"

"Let me see! Wow! Baby, your hands feel cold! And your fingers are stiff! You are acting like…No! No, no, no, no! you can't be! Please, baby, talk to me."

"Hello, 9-1-1? Can you send somebody? Please, send somebody quick. My baby…I mean my wife, she won't talk to me!" "Is she what?!" "I'm not going to even entertain that thought. Just make her talk to me!"

Roy Lee 'Simon' Jarmon

MY DARLING ROY

[20000530TU1130A]

My Darling Roy,
First and foremost –
I love you.
Thank you for being
My strength when I
Am weak, thank you for
Making me smile when
I want to cry.
Thank you for sticking with
Me thru thick and thin.
Thank you for being a great
Daddy to our son.
Thank you for being my
Lover and my friend.

You are my hero.

Thanks
For being the wind beneath
My wings.
With Appreciation,
"Me"

Written to me by my late wife, Nathalyn Vershelle Cato Jarmon

GOD IS THE KEY

(Written for and presented to our son, Erick Russell Hunt,
on his graduation and morning into the world of manhood via the
ORIDA program performed at Ebenezer Baptist Church)

Our dearest son, Erick, we want to offer or present to you a few key words of wisdom and encouragement as you cross over the threshold into manhood and venture out into this big, wide world. What we want you to remember most is that <u>God is the Key!</u>

We all know that there are trials and temptations awaiting you. This is a given. Nonetheless, the obstacles that you will encounter will not determine whether you will reach your goal. That accomplishment will be decided or determined by you. Just make sure that you remember that <u>God is the Key!</u>

It is not the obstacles that you encounter – but your attitude towards those obstacles – that matters. Yes, <u>ATTITUDE</u> is a very important part of the puzzle. Philippians 4:13 states for us that *we can do all things through Christ, who strengthens us.* Son, <u>God is the Key!</u>

Another way to approach this endeavor is by utilizing the acronym <u>LIFE</u>: L-I-F-E. The "L" must stand for <u>LOVE</u>. For Christ says in John 15:12 *that this is my commandment, that you love another as I have loved you.*

The "I" stands for <u>INTEGRITY</u>. Integrity is the essence of who you are. Are you honest? Can you be trusted? Are you trustworthy? And no one can answer these questions but you. These are questions that can only be answered by the way in which you live your life. And that must be in an upright way because Proverbs 11:3 tells us that *the integrity of the upright will guide them, but the perverseness of the unfaithful will destroy them.* And Titus 2:6-8 says *"Likewise exhort the young men to be sober-minded, in all things showing yourself to be a pattern of good works; in doctrine showing integrity, reverence, incorruptibility, such speech that cannot be condemned, that one who is an opponent may be ashamed, having nothing evil to say of you."*

The letter "F" stands for FOCUS. In that, I mean 'Focus on God'. When you keep your focus on God, you do not live for the moment or what fad is happening at the time. Instead, you will keep in mind his commandments and be obedient to his Word. For when you are under the umbrella of God, the world cannot dictate the outcome. For 1John 4:4 tells us that *you are of God, little children, and have overcome them, because He who is in you is greater than he who is in the world.*

The "E" in LIFE stands for <u>ETERNAL</u>. Not only does God's word give you a prescription for living abundantly here on earth, but He (Christ) saves our souls from Hell. John 3:16 states *"For God so loved the world that He gave his only begotten son, that whoever believes in Him shall not perish but have everlasting life".*

So, when Christ returns, He will carry us back with Him because He has gone and prepared a place for us. We will reign forever with Him instead of having a life of eternal damnation.

With this speech, we are to give you some type of medallion symbolizing your new journey. Our medallion or medal that we chose for you is this ring. This ring is a symbol of Jesus as He encircles us. Remember, as long as you are encircled by Him and his commandments, whatever obstacles that come up against you cannot stand.

Yes, my Son, <u>God is the Key</u>. So, with this medal – this ring – I give to you at this time. Because it's a ring, you can wear it on your finger. But for this moment, however, I chose to present this token to you on this golden chain. And for now, I shall put the chain around your neck and allow this ring to fall over your heart where Jesus and His Word shall live. And in Him you shall always – no matter what the trial or obstacle – be successful in all your endeavors. Yes, my Son, <u>God is the Key</u>.

Roy Lee 'Simon' Jarmon

AN AFFIRMATION FROM GOPPY

(Written to accompany my God-Daughter's
(Laresa Tene Jett) Birthday card)

Do you sometimes feel that I don't love you?
    Or, maybe, that I don't care?
When you reach over the many miles
    And don't find anyone there?

When your phone calls are not readily answered
    Or not immediately returned?
Do you feel like your letters are unread
    And all your cards are burned?

It's because I'm always on the move,
    Which makes my life unruly.
That's why it takes so long in letting you know
    That I really do love you truly.

When I got your Father's Day card, my heart
    Jumped – I felt so proud.
I ran around showing it to everyone!
    I was floating on a cloud.

I remember when you first came into my life
    And for that, I still pray:
Thanking the Lord for you, my dearest –
    My Godchild named Tene.

Saturday, August 01, 1998 @3:30 PM

by

Roy Lee "Simon" Jarmon (Goppy)

THANK YOU

*[This was written to me by my Godson BJ. Written to me following the
death of my wife, Nathalyn Vershelle Cato Jarmon,
who was his beloved Godmother]*

by
ALVIN BERNARD (BJ) REW II

You are always there for me
Whether it's good or bad.
You always make me smile
Whether I'm sad or mad.
"Stand tall and stand strong
You have to live on."
I was weak, but you gave me the strength to move on.
You are the house on this ground.
You stand strong, properly.
One day I'll stand strong
And you'll be proud of me.
I can make it through the bad weather.
You are like glue. You are going to keep me together.
When Gommy left, I went to the back and cried.
But you were there.
They tried to break me but they couldn't;
No matter how hard they tried.
That's just one time – probably a million more.
17 years of rain from your knowledge;
And when it rains, it pours
On top of me. I start to rot when I go astray.
I can't live on bread alone. I need your water to intake.
Because of you, I see what I'm supposed to do.
I guess all I'm trying to do is say, "Thank you."

Merry Christmas!

LYRESHIA'S LETTER OF RECOMMENDATION

April 22, 2014

I am delighted to write this letter of recommendation on behalf of Lyreshia Hailstork, a young woman with much drive and determination. She would not only be an asset to your law degree program, but to the entire law profession as well.

Among the many exemplary qualities Lyreshia possesses, I choose to point out the following ones: Focused, ambitious, hardworking, industrious, courageous, and bright. Might I quickly state that these are qualities not very prevalent among young people in Miss Hailstrok's age group?

As a former high school teacher, I observed the work of hundreds of students. None impressed me as much as Lyreshia. She took such care and pride in her work as she prepared her reports and completed her daily studies. While other students may have been satisfied with doing enough to get by, Lyreshia would settle for nothing less than a "B".

As a landlord, I watch Lyreshia work two and sometimes three jobs while attending college full-time. The diligent 6-year pursuit of her studies in spite of tremendous financial struggles and personal hardships evidences her courage, Inner strength, and perseverance. While others may have taken the easy way out and given up, Lyreshia pushed harder and worked harder. Her confidence did not wane.

Miss Hailstork has the ability to be a team player while at the same time maintaining a sense of individualism. She will take a stand for what she believes is right and not compromise her values or her integrity. There are qualities that I, as training manager for AT&T over twenty years, did not observe often in the adults that worked in the company. To observe them in Lyreshia is outstanding.

In summary, Lyreshia Hailstork has been able to transform her humble beginnings into a bright, promising future through drive, determination, and hard work. She is a young woman of good character, substance, and great possibilities – the field of law or any profession stands to benefit.

I recommend that Lyreshia Hailstork be accepted into your law program without reservation.

N. Vershelle Jarmon
President and Owner,
Melodies by Shelley

THOUGHTS OF THE COMING
2002 FAMILY REUNION

Well over a year has come and gone
Since last – together – we sang our song
Of what we shouldn't and what we should;
Of family ties and brotherhood;
The gaiety of laughter while hugging and kissing;
The tears of joy, the thoughts of missing
The ones we love and hold so dear –
Of those that are far and others so near.
It's hurriedly approaching our next yearly meeting.
That's why I'm sending you all these greetings.
There's no need to compare: neither better nor least.
Just make your way to this coast on the East.

Roy Lee 'Simon' Jarmon

Spiritual Inspiration

HE

I know you think you've got it made
With all your money and wealth,
But I know of only one man, my friend,
Who've really conquered Death.

Now, you may tell me that he's dead –
That they hung Him on the cross.
And if you really think He's dead, my friend,
Then I'm afraid you're lost.

You say He's made only idle promises
That never will come true.
But I must tell you He's alive in me,
And He can live in you.

Roy Lee 'Simon' Jarmon

MEN WHY ARE YOU HIDING

(This speech was written and presented at an afternoon Chruch's "Men's and Women's Day Program")

Men, why are you hiding? Are you scared? Are you afraid? If so, of what? Of who? You must be hiding because I see so very few of you. Everywhere I go, there are so few of you. Of me. Of us. There are always plenty of women around. Plenty of females. Plenty of ladies. But I always find myself asking, "Where are all the men? Where are they hiding?"

Let's take a look at man. What is a man? David asked this question in the 8th Psalm scripture where he states (in paraphrase): "When I think of the heavens, the moon and the stars created by only your hands and your fingers! The beasts of the field, the fowls of the air, and the fish of the sea. Your creation, Lord (as well as me)! And you place all this at my feet and tell man to rule it. To control it. To protect it. For thou hast made Man a little lower than the angels."

William Shakespeare said in Hamlet II, 2, 13, "(Man) in action, how like an angel! In appearance, how like a god! The BEAUTY of the world!"

John Donne stated in his <u>Devotions</u>, "No man is an Island, entire of itself; every man is a piece of the continent, a part of the main." So, I feel we should do as Mr. Schweitzer did when he said in his <u>Civilization and Ethics</u>, "Hunt, then, for some situation in which your humanity may be used."

And, of course, Arthur Miller believed in his <u>Death of a Salesman</u>, "(Man) is not the finest character that ever lived. But he's a human being, a terrible thing is happening to him."

And we see that Pascal wrote "(Man) is the GLORY *and* SHAME of the universe."

<u>Opinion</u>: How, then, can man be the GLORY *and* SHAME of the universe? What is this terrible thing that's happening to him? I would like to say that maybe nothing's bad is happening to him; just maybe nothing good has happened to him yet.

I know that some of you have been here all day. You're tired. You're ready to leave. You keep looking at your watch. The clock on the wall! Trying to see what time it is. Well, what time is it?

In the 3rd chapter of Ecclesiastes, it states that there is a time for all things. A time to be born, a time to die, a time to plant, a time to harvest, a time to build up, a time to heal, to cry, to laugh, to love. What time do you have?

Robert Herrick wrote in his <u>To the Virgins:</u>
>Gather your rose buds while you may,
>>Old time is still a-flying,
>And this same flower that smiles today,
>>Tomorrow will be dying.

<u>Opinion</u>: Tomorrow is not promised to you. Can't you see what it is? No! don't look at your watch. Don't look at the clock on the wall! Look in your heart to see what time it is! And my heart says that the time is NOW! Can't you see that, too? Everyone in this building should be wise enough to see that.

Speaking of wisdom, I'm reminded of Walt Whitman, where he wrote in his <u>Song of the Open Road,</u> "Wisdom is not finally tested in the schools,...but is of the soul." And the 10th verse of the 111th Psalm tells us, "The fear of the Lord is the beginning of wisdom."

<u>Opinion</u>: Why, then, are men hiding? I would like to say that it's because they don't have the wisdom to know what time it is. And they don't have time to realize man's purpose on this Earth. We are here to oversee God's creation. And that's a job that needs all of our time, and there's no way that we can have the wisdom to make the right decision unless we fear the Lord. Unless God enters our hearts, our minds, our lives. And the time is now.

Being that this is a Men's and Women's Day program, I feel that it would not be complete unless I mention man's relationship with woman. For she is part of Man! Made from the rib in his side.

Think about that. From his side. Not from a bone in his foot. Meaning that she is not to be kicked around like a football, nor walked on and trampled like an old worn-out rug. But from his side to be at his side.

Neither was she made from a bone in his head. Signifying that she is not the head and should not become the head. She's not to lead you, Man. She's from your side to be at your side.

And this brings to mind Robert Burns "Henpecked Husband" which goes:

> Cursed be the man, the poorest wretch in life,
> The crouching vessel to the tyrant wife,
> Who has no will but in her high permission;
> Who has not sixpence but in her possession;
> Who must to her his dear friend's secret tell;
> Who dreads a curtain lecture worse than hell.
> Were such the wife fallen to my part,
> I'd break her spirit or I'd break her heart.

Thank you for listening. And if you were really listening, you'll realize that the time really is NOW!

Roy Lee 'Simon' Jarmon

PURITY

1 Timothy 4:12 (<u>International Standard Version</u>) says to me, "Do not let anyone look down on you because you are young, but be an example for other believers in your speech, behavior, love, faithfulness, and purity.

My hope was to focus on the single characteristic 'purity'. And in my contemplation on how to present this topic 'purity', I thought to bring an example of something pure and extrapolate from that item's traits. However, I couldn't find a thing in this world that fits the description. Not a thing in this world.

Now this enigma brought a few questions to mind. First of all, what is 'purity'? What does it mean? What's the definition of 'purity'?

One definition defines purity as – free from contamination by dross or evil. Contamination means to make impure by contact or mixture. Dross is defined as waste products or impurities; worthless material; rubbish. And we define evil as morally bad or wrong; harmful. That which causes misfortunes, suffering, etc.

That's asking quite a bit, don't you think? Now, the second question arises: how in the world can a person be pure? Well, the answer to that question is, "You can't".

Now that I've said that, let me explain. Wait! Wait! Wait, let me explain myself. Remember that no example of purity exists in the world. So, let's see! Shall I approach it scientifically or religiously? Let me start with the religious approach first, okay?

James 1:27 states (<u>New Living Translation</u>) Pure and genuine religion in the sight of God the Father means caring for orphans and widows in their distress and refusing to let the world corrupt you. But this doesn't mean that we are pure. Fortunately, the Lord has provided a plan of purification for us. You must be born again. As Christ told Nicodemus in John 3:3 (King James Bible), Jesus answered and said unto him, Verily, verily, I say unto thee, except a man be born again, he cannot see the kingdom of God.

Okay! Let's say that we get born again! But does that mean that we are pure? I am sure we can all offer our arguments for or against, depending on how one defines the word "pure" or "purity". After all, purity is a process and not a state of being. In order to strive toward purity, one must allow God to dwell within them daily because all purity is in God.

For instance, let's observe the following scriptures. In Psalms 119:140, we find these words (King James Version) Thy word is very pure: therefore, thy servant loveth it. Psalms 19:8 (King James Version) The statutes of the LORD are right, rejoicing the heart: the commandment of the LORD is pure, enlightening the eyes. James 3:17 tells us (English Standard Version) But the wisdom from above is first pure, then peaceable, gentle, open to reason, full of mercy and good fruits, impartial and sincere.

Now, then, we find purity in God's word, his wisdom, and his commandments. But let's not forget our mediator Christ Jesus, for without Him we are lost. It's only through Him that we will get to see our Heavenly Father. For Jesus said to Thomas in John 14:6 (English Standard Version), "I am the way, and the truth, and the life. No one comes to the Father except through me." And Acts 16:31 we see (New Living Translation) They replied, "Believe in the Lord Jesus and you will be saved, along with everyone in your household."

Through the blood of Jesus, we are purified as recorded in 1 John 3:3 (New American Standard Version). And everyone who has this hope fixed on Him purifies himself, just as He is pure. And it's necessary to be pure if we want to see our heavenly Father. In Matthew 5:8 we read (International Standard Version) "How blessed are those who are pure in heart, because it is they who will see God!" and Psalms 24:3-4 (English Standard Version) Who shall ascend the hill of the LORD? And who shall stand in his holy place? He who has clean hands and a pure heart, who does not lift up his soul to what is false and does not swear deceitfully.

That's what He has said, and that's good enough for me. As you can see, I dismissed the scientific side of the argument. I concentrated mainly concerning or dealing with the religious aspects through the scriptures. And why did I do that? Why did I deal only with the Christian side? Well, I'll tell you! I'll tell you why! Once I finished discussing the religious and scriptural side, it hit me! It hit me like a ton of bricks – to quote a well-known phrase. I realized that if I follow and live pure, as in the scriptures, then nothing else matters. Though there may be worldly defined algorithms and formulas for purity, none seemed to measure up to God's Word and plan.

So, what's the need to digress? Why discuss the lesser argument? Why go there when God's plan supersedes all others? And I choose to concentrate on the higher calling. If I can – and He says I can – be pure through Him, then (for me) that's all that matters.

Roy Lee 'Simon' Jarmon

TO YOU, WORLD

You should admire a man like Christ.
To save you, World, He gave his life.
King did it, and Kennedy too.
I'd give mine if I thought it would do.
If I thought it would help, I'd be first on the menu
To change you, World. Well, the people in you.

Roy Lee 'Simon' Jarmon

THANKS LORD FOR THE HEAT WAVE

I was listening to the radio
And I heard the weatherman say,
"The temperature has exceeded
Over a hundred degrees again today!
It's lasted over a month in Texas."
Some have said that it came from hexes.

It's been so dry
That I've heard a farmer cry,
"My cattle are about to die!

My poultry farm
Has been wiped out",
Is what I heard another one shout!
His frustrations were easy to see,
As this other man spoke to me:
"I've planted and planted,
But I'll have you to know
That it's just too dry
To make things grow.
The crop that's up can't survive.
It's too darn hot to keep them alive."

Heat exhaustion has caused many strokes;
Still, I've heard,
"It's just a hoax."
To me it's drought
And famine depicted
As my Holy Bible predicted.

Thank you, Lord,
For this heat wave.
It's given me strength.
It's made me brave.
I've been living and serving
You, Lord, with a sigh;
But now it's nearing your return
And I feel it's very, very nigh.

Roy Lee 'Simon' Jarmon

THE SALVATION PLAN

Sure, it's important to have confidence in one's self. And yes, one should be proud of being who he or she is. Be positive and do the best that you can do. Be the best 'you' that you can be. But I recall a statement that <u>Martin Luther King, Jr.</u> made in one of his speeches that says "<u>There is some good in the worst of us and some evil in the best of us. When we discover this, we are less prone to hate our enemies.</u>" In that reasoning, as well as others, we must recognize the fact that we are all flawed.

Since we are all flawed, it stands to reason that there must or a need for a standard for some type of measurement to determine man's salvation. I am aware that there are those who believe, and choose a religion that says, that you can do a good enough job to save yourself. But being good is not enough to save oneself. After all, the statement above suggests that some of the most hideous, vile, and evil persons throughout history have some bad within them. And that's the dilemma.

I do tend to agree with the validity of Mr. King's statement. Therein lies the rub! Then, how can man save himself if there is evil in the best of us? I dare say one can't. But I do have a solution for the salvation of man. How can it be solved? How can it be determined? Well, to be truthful, it's not my solution. It's God's Salvation Plan.

The Plan of God's Salvation may be stated in three sentences. The first states that every man is lost in sin and cannot save himself, as suggested in John 6:44. Then the second sentence says that God has provided complete salvation for sinners through Jesus Christ. And, finally, the third one is that whosoever will repent of sin and accept Christ as his own Savior receives this salvation.

Furthermore, let me reemphasize the fact that Salvation is provided by God. There is nothing that man can do to save himself. It was because man was hopelessly lost in sin that God moved to give him this salvation.

Now, why would God do that? If we are sinners and have turned our backs on God, then why would he want to offer this salvation? There is one reason only! **Love**! God loves you! And how do I know that, you may ask? Look at the scripture John 3:16 (KJV), which reads "For God so loved the world, that he gave his only begotten Son, that whosoever believeth in him should not perish, but have everlasting life". We also see in Romans 5:8 (KJV) "But God commendeth his love toward us, in that, while we were yet sinners, Christ died for us".

Surely this is an unusual love! This is a love that we find only in the Divine heart of God. The Apostle Paul wrote in Ephesians 1:4-5 (KJV) "According as he hath chosen us in him before the foundation of the world, that we should be holy and without blame before him in love: Having predestined us unto the adoption of children by Jesus Christ to himself, according to the good pleasure of his will".

At first, this may seem that God chooses those who are saved to do His will and His works. If that was the case, we could just leave this to His wisdom and Justine and go about our business as if nothing happened to us, by us, or for us.

But it seems limited and questionable to me. And God is not a god of confusion. Nor, by no means, is He limited. So, who are the saved? If we look back at John 3:16, we see that the Word says 'whosoever will'. This means that anyone who comes and believes in Christ and that God has raised Him from the dead, can and will be saved.

Furthermore, if we take a further look at what the scriptures are saying, I believe that God's Salvation is an offer of Grace. 'By Grace' we mean that it is a gift. Not earned. Not purchased. For if we look at the scripture Ephesians 2:8-9 (NKJV), we find these words: "For by grace you have been saved through faith, and that not of yourselves; it is the gift of God, not of works, lest anyone should boast". The Savior was God's gift. Salvation is a gift. Redemption is bestowed upon us without money, stratification, or price.

But Grace means even more than this. It is a gift that is not deserved. God did not give us His Son because we were worthy of deserving. We were lost and helpless and utterly without any merit of our own. God loved us and offered us salvation freely, in spite of the fact that we do not deserve it. Now, that's GRACE!

And another thing, Salvation is made possible by the Atonement of Jesus Christ. Atonement means the paying for our sins by the Savior. Man has been separated from God by sin. The whole truth, according to the Scriptures, is that Christ took our place as a sinner, and suffered in our stead; taking all the punishment that we deserve because of our sin; and, because he was the Son of God, his sacrifice is sufficient for all who trust in Him. We can think of his work, therefore, as a sacrifice, as a substitute, and as sufficient.

In Isaiah 53:5-6 (KJV), we find "But he was wounded for our transgressions, he was bruised for our iniquities: the chastisement of our peace was upon him; and with his stripes we are healed. All we like sheep have gone astray; we have turned every one to his own way; and the Lord hath laid on him the iniquity of us all". And 2 Corinthians 5:21 (KJV) tells us that For he hath made him to be sin for us, who knew no sin; that we might be made the righteousness of God in him. Likewise, in 1 Peter 3:18 (KJV), "For Christ also hath once suffered for sins, the just for the unjust, that he might bring us to God, being put to death in the flesh, but quickened by the Spirit".

The Atonement was a substitutionary sacrifice. To deny that is to deny the whole gospel. Without that, there is no way of cleansing from sin. So, then, Salvation must be accepted by man. For in Luke 13:4 (King James Bible) we read "I tell you, Nay: but except ye repent, ye shall all likewise perish". And in John 8:24, the scriptures tell us (International Standard Version), "That is why I told you that you will die in your sins, for unless you believe that I am, you'll die in your sins."

So, in accepting Salvation, we find that Christ asked us to repent and believe in Him. Then, Repentance is also a part of Salvation. In the scripture Psalm 38:18, we find these words (New Living Translation), "But I confess my sins; I am deeply sorry for what I have done". And the scripture in 2 Corinthians 7:10 reads (New Living Translation) "For the kind of sorrow God wants us to experience leads us away from sin and results in salvation. There's no regret for that kind of sorrow. But worldly sorrow, which lacks repentance, results in spiritual death".

Repentance, then, is sorrow for sin that will lead one to forsake it – to turn his back on sin and his face toward God.

The second condition is Faith in Christ. So one must admit that Jesus came as God's Son to suffer and die for lost sinners, to admit that he is able to save all who will trust him, and to admit that he is the only one who can save. For Jesus said himself, "He that believeth not hath already been judged, because he hath not believed on the name of the only begotten Son of God" according to John 3:18.

Before closing, let me say a word about baptism. First, why be baptized? Checking in the books of Matthew, Mark, Luke, and the Acts of the Apostles in the New Testament, Christ commanded us to be baptized in the name of the Father, the Son, and the Holy Spirit.

Secondly, how shall we be baptized? For this answer, let's take a look at Matthew 3:16 and Mark 1:9, referring to the baptism of Jesus by John the Baptist in the river Jordan. There is no doubt that Jesus was submerged beneath the water, and after the baptism, the Bible stated that He "came up out of the water". Also, refer to Acts 8:36-39 when Philip baptized the eunuch, it says, "...they both went down into the water, both Philip and the eunuch; and he baptized him. And when they came up out of the water, the Spirit of the Lord caught away Philip; and the eunuch saw him no more..." And to erase further doubt, listen to Paul in Romans 6:3-5, which states "Know ye not, that so many of us as were baptized into Jesus Christ were baptized into his death? Therefore, we are buried with Him into death: that like as Christ was raised up from the dead by the glory of the Father, even so we also should walk in newness of life. For if we have been planted together in the likeness of his death, we shall be also in the likeness of his resurrection". And, too, Colossians 2:12 says to us "Having been buried with Him in baptism, wherein ye were also raised with Him through faith in the working of God, who raised Him from the dead."

This symbolized the burial of Christ himself, after He died for our sins on the cross, and His resurrection on the third day, as well as a resurrection from the grave and a life hereafter.

Finally, who shall be baptized? This ordinance (baptism) is not intended to save, but for those who are already saved. Meaning those who have first believed in Christ and have trusted in Him as their own personal Savior. This doesn't seem to include infants or babies. Nor does it seem to leave room for baptism by proxy. I feel that baptism is for those who have believed and been saved from their sins through Christ. Nobody else is eligible. Nobody!

To God be the Power, the Honor, and the Glory. Thank you, my Heavenly Father, for your unconditional Love and Compassion by which you provided us this divine Salvation Plan.

Roy Lee 'Simon' Jarmon

CHRISTMAS TIME

The weather has become a risk.
The wind is blowing quite brisk
And beating like a whisk.
Christmas is on its way

Outside my window, all is white.
Snow has fallen during the night.
Birds have already taken their flight.
Christmas is on its way.

That's all well and good, and yet
There's one thing we shouldn't forget –
CHRIST is the one who paid the debt.
Only in **HIM** is there Christmas time.

Roy Lee 'Simon' Jarmon

Daily
"Slices Of Life's"
Excursions

ROLLING ALONG, ALONE

I've now become a freak.
My strong mind is weak.
I'm a cripple man
That no one can stand
But I…
    I keep rolling along, alone.

My head's full of phobias and fears.
I'm offered only liquors and beers.
My mind's clouded with smudges and smears.
My eyes are strained and loaded with tears
Because I get no cheers.
But I…
    I keep rolling along, alone.

I'm not handsome
Because I'm in this chair.
I'm a little twisted
But I have pretty hair.
They don't like my looks,
But I know my books.
But I'm not really smart
Because I have a broken heart.
I'm not muscular.
I'm quite puny.
When I talk philosophically,
They call me loony.
I'm just a cripple man
That no one can stand,
But I…
    I keep rolling along, alone.

Roy Lee 'Simon' Jarmon

PURPOSE OF LIFE

What is the purpose of life?
Is it to be confronted,
    All of our days
        With worldly evils of desire
    That confounds us
        In such lustful
        And tempting ways?
Or
    Shall we douse the fire?

Is it that we are to be
Pets of experimentation
    Whose purpose is to reek
        From the odors of annihilation
    (so to speak)?

Is it something that just happens along
    Solely for the purpose of living?
Or
    Is it only for dismays –
        Constant kindness: always forgiving?
Or
Can all the above be wrong
And
    'Death'
        The important phase?

Roy Lee 'Simon' Jarmon

PRISONER AT THE TOP

I climbed to the mountain top,
And placed the crown upon my head.
I sat down, crossed my legs,
And looked down upon my stead.

Now I was safe from poverty's pinch,
And all that poverty could bring.
I have no fear of those dreaded diseases:
They wouldn't dare bother a king.

As I glanced around, they all seemed sick.
They gagged and sneezed and coughed.
So I ordered my royal army to get
Busy and kill them off.

My army killed every sickly frame,
And not a one let out a cry.
The dead bodies covered the ground,
But the diseases did not die.

The disease continued to march forward.
I ordered my army again.
But, this time, only my royal army
Was dead, lifeless, slain.

As they continued to march on and on,
I yelled and yelled, "Go back!"
I hollered, screamed and shouted but
Continuously marched that wave of black.

Exactly ten feet from the center they sat
In a circle: all around.
They sat and stared lifeless and weird:
No wink, no smile, no frown.

I tried to find out what they wanted,
But they didn't make a sound.
Then I realized that they had what they wanted:
A kingdom, a thorn, a crown.

Roy Lee 'Simon' Jarmon

THE BEACH

I like to visit the cool,
Sandy beach at dawn
And watch the sky
Gradually come
To life
As if someone is slowly turning on
A dimmer switch.
I become excited when I see
That brilliant, orange-colored ball
Floating into view.
As it peeks its head
Above the horizon
And slowly rises over the calm,
Flat,
Glass-smooth ocean,
Its penetrating warmth seems
To seep into my every pore
And dissolves away all my tiredness
From early risings.

Roy Lee 'Simon' Jarmon

COMMUNICATION

Thousands of years ago
when only the scribes did most of the reading and writing,
There were very limited areas
or pockets of communication.
Then came the printing press
And, now,
words could be poured
onto paper
in a much quicker fashion.
There were newspapers
and books everywhere,
But – according to today's standards –
Traveling to the places of information
was at a snail's crawl.
With today's technology
And the utilization of cellphones
fax machines,
email,
texts and Instagram
communication happens instantaneously –
In a flash.

Roy Lee 'Simon' Jarmon

IN WAITING

<u>Good things come</u>
<u>To those who wait…</u>
I waited,
    And waited
    And nothing came
    To me
        (That was good)
        On time
To help.

<u>But don't wait</u>
<u>Too long…</u>
I must have waited
    Too long.
    It's time
    I strive
    And make things
        Happen for myself.

I worked,
And strove,
And made
Ends meet.
I retired,
    Settling (only)
        For success.

Then I returned
To waiting
    Again,

And,
>   That, what I'd been waiting for,
>>   Became
Manifest.

Roy Lee 'Simon' Jarmon

TIED TO A SUPER EGO

it seems such a shame that
some mothers and daughters –
in their forgetful thoughtlessness –
are married to each other
instead of their
(shall I say) supposedly
significant other.

of course, they
must egotistically love
them. it's almost
(i would say assuredly)
as if they don't
have a choice of letting them go
without losing
a piece of themselves.

however, I feel
that a great number
of individuals
have a distorted view
of the true meaning
of love. sure they may
(they can and will
be emphatic about, too)
give you many reasons why
they think that they are right.

love, in many of us,
is represented as

possessiveness
projected in an obsessive
manner for the purpose of
manipulation
to a self-gratifying agenda.

    and whether you want to
accept the truth,
or not, that is
the exact opposite
of <u>LOVE!</u> which is
freedom in itself.

    but, we ostracize
the truth
and search for
rationale
to support our disagreements
while we remain slaves:
tied to a super EGO.

Roy Lee 'Simon' Jarmon

SHE DANCED

She danced before me
    As a flirtatious coquette –
    Enchanting and seductive.
I gazed – not startled but –
    Hypnotic and watched her
    Gossamer gown; white
    As snow and (it seemed)
    Just as light.
I could feel – deep
    Inside my soul –
    A growing. A swell
    That I knew
    Could and would
    Control me.
I – without knowing if
    It was permissible –
    Reached, in slow motion,
    Even if just to touch
    Her sheer garment's hem.
I simultaneously felt
    A piercing, burning pain
    That jolted me awake.
The room was filled
    With smoke and
    I managed to escape
    With only a badly
    Burned hand.
If she had worn
    BLACK, I'm sure
    I would have recognized

And ignored her.
Anyhow, I find myself
    exceedingly glad that –
    on this night –
    DEATH wore white.

Roy Lee 'Simon' Jarmon

WHILE TRAVELING

While traveling down life's highway,
Sometimes you may have to run
In querying about the time.
Other times you'll glide along your way
Having loads and worlds of fun
With stress quite sublime.

And sometimes you might stumble
Or maybe, even fall
Over something you didn't see.
But don't lie there and grumble,
But get back on the ball
And continue on your journey.

There may come a thunderstorm
With you caught in the middle –
Cold and soaking wet.
But farther along you can get warm
Where (under the beautiful fiddle)
You just may win your bet.

Roy Lee 'Simon' Jarmon

SHE'S REALLY HAPPY, NOW

We met.
We smiled.
We talked and laughed.
I asked for an invitation
and got it.
I asked for her time
And she willingly gave.

I arrived.
We kissed.
I sat and she served.
She wanted me to be speedy;
I wanted to cruise.
I asked for her heart
and she offered her hand.

She was ready
for anything
that she agreed on,
but we were
not in agreement.
I asked for her body.
and she wanted my soul.

She wanted me there.
I left.
She asked me back.
I didn't return.
She tried. I didn't.
She cried. I didn't.
But she's really happy, now.

Roy Lee 'Simon' Jarmon

SO MUST MAN

Man shouldn't be like a limb
that's caught in a whim –
as in a swiftly flowing stream –
when trying to follow a dream
lest he aimlessly glide
[dipping and darting
from side to side]
depending on the current's strength to go.
You may say, "Going with the flow!"
But the streamlined stone
that's sitting in the middle
doesn't have to go along –
playing the fiddle –
stumbling and staggering, but parts the wave.
(There's a difference between
Being foolish and brave.)
The rock redirects the head-on force
and guides it around himself, of course.
Like the rock must stand sublime,
so must man in calculating time.

Roy Lee 'Simon' Jarmon

I BELONG – AT THE COMPANY PICNIC

"Good, Lord! What's that?" she shouted with a chuckle.

"Some representative you are. You're over an hour late. I don't know what to do with you now. Maybe 50 lashes with a wet noodle will do it, you think?"

"I don't think it's a good idea to give me a hard time at this picnic this afternoon," I said with a shrug of confidence.

"And why is that?" she asked smilingly while looking around at the other ladies at the picnic table?

"Well, all I can say is…take a look at my hat!".

It was an almost blinding, bright yellow with a half bill and a small snowball on top. It had etched across the front in Dingy (formerly white) dog-chewed letters 'Meaner than a Junk Yard Dog!'.

Laughing heartedly, she managed to blurt out, "That's pretty mean".

"Of course," I assured them "I am not that mean. I only mean what I say. And I must say that here, at this table, is the most beautiful and Intellectual group of ladies in this company."

"Why, thank you very much!" they said in unison.

"But, excuse me now, ladies. I'm going to get me a burger and a dog."

"Alright, Simon" she said as they looked around at each other as I walked away.

I knew that they were still giggling as I strolled off and imagined the whispers,

The stares and the laughter. And I thought to myself, "Nonetheless, I am a part.

I belong!"

Roy Lee 'Simon' Jarmon

MY WIFE IS NOT AN UNKIND LADY

My Wife is not an unkind lady –
      Not unkind at all.
Society just demands dual,
      Contradicting roles;
That's all!

See, ladies and gentlemen.
    I, too,
      Am a person of kindness.
I really happened to need that woman –
    That woman of mine(ness).

But do I love her?
    What a question:
      Of course!
It would tear my heart to pieces
    If you grant her a divorce.

That would mean no more US.
That would mean no more fuss.
That would mean no more necking,
And no more "Oh, what the heck(ing)".
No more scheming, cheating, lying.
No more "It's your turn! The baby's crying!"
No more "Get out! Get your hat!"
No more this. No more that.

She didn't only tease and use me.
    Not always was she sarcastic.
She, often enough, pleased but fooled me,

And sometimes she was quite drastic.
At first I called it nagging,
  But then it became a part of me.
And now I'm truly saying that
  Deep down, it's in this heart of me.

She does it because she loves me.
  That's the only reason.
She doesn't have insane flashes,
  And it matters not what the season.

It's only her background environment:
  No confidence! (- a must.)
No faith in other people.
  You know...
      The things that make one trust.

All the while I'm home, she hollers,
  "I know you've been deceiving me!"
No matter how I swear I don't
  She never ends up believing me.

So, she tries one thing after another
  And always ends up yelling.
If only I can get her to see
  That's it's the truth I'm telling.

And once she almost believed me,
  But I need more time, of course.
Then LOVE and HAPPINESS! Forever.
  So, please, don't grant her divorce.

Roy Lee 'Simon' Jarmon

MASCULINITY AT ITS FINEST

Do you know what time I went to bed last night?
Seven! That's right, seven.
Do you know what time I went to sleep?
Eleven! That's right, eleven.
Four hours I lay there
    thinking of Hell and Heaven.
Hell! That's tight, and Heaven.
I'm a man and there are few of us.
Compared to women we're one to seven.
One! That's right, to seven.
There's a women for every day of the week.
And you can find them if you'll only seek.
There's one for Monday, Tuesday, Wednesday,
Thursday, Friday, Saturday, and Sunday.
A different lady to make every night a FUN day.
All night long allow her to
    hug you, squeeze you, and kiss you.
Leave here saturated with infatuation
    not knowing that for a week she'll miss you.
Change them like you do your underwear –
    a different one each day.
Lead them on and use them.
You know what to do and say.
So, go on Man, and grab you one.
Grab! That's right, you one.
And have some fun.
Thaaat's right, you son-of-a-gun.
Even if your week increases to thirteen days,
    don't worry about enough ladies:
They'll keep on having babies.

But, if they stop having babies,
    you can have my entitled six.
Now, don't think for a moment
    that I'll be in a fix.
Encircled in a woman's arms,
    I know that's Heaven to you.
Encircled in a woman's arms
    is heavenly. I know that's true.
Encircled in a woman's arms
    is Heaven to me too.
But if one woman wants to hold me
    every night of the week, then,
        for me, one woman will do.
One woman! That's right, for me will do.
As many women as you can get
    is a lesson for you to heed.
But one woman who really loves me
    is all I need.
One woman! That's right, who really loves me
    is all I need.

Roy Lee 'Simon' Jarmon

Military Inspirations - Healing Wounds

THE FOXHOLE

A foxhole – though it may appear small,
Cramped, and claustrophobic – can
Contain a universe of its own.

There is only on way in and one way out –
A peephole existence and exit.
    This has a tendency to narrow one's view.

Although the intent of the foxhole is to have your back
Protected by friendly fire,
You can never be absolutely sure.

When bombs are exploding around you
And darkness is your only shield,
The situation can play many mental tricks on a soldier's mind.

As long as one is fighting in battle
And the bodies are falling around you like cut weeds,
You can react and remain okay.

When bullets are zinging through the air
And whistling past your head,
You fight and cope.

While the guns are thundering
And the smell of burnt gunpowder smoke is in the air,
You utilize your instincts, and you find that you are surviving.
    But it's the silence that frightens.

When you hear no sound except the pounding of your heartbeat;
As it grows louder and louder
To a thundering, roaring thump within your chest and
In your dry, parched throat;
Now that's when the universe of the
Foxhole comes into play – in your mind.
That's when one really becomes afraid.

Then comes the fight! The real fight –
As has happened on too many occasions –
Is the fright that comes from the enemy within one's own self
And not from the enemy from without.

Roy Lee 'Simon' Jarmon

I CAUGHT MYSELF SMILING

I came to myself.
I was sitting there at the computer
Staring into oblivion.

I was daydreaming – reminiscing –
About our first skirmish at Ankay Pass.
The Vietnamese hit us hard. They hit us fast.
Yes, Charlie hit us heavy that day.
On our right side was a steep mountain range –
Straight up. On our left – straight down.
There was no place to go
To get out of the beating zone.
As I was crawling from the thicket
Of briars and stickers on the edge of the pass –
From which I had dove into –
I noticed that the American was crippled
On the driver's side rear.
The feeder was dead and the gunner
Of the Quad-50 was bleeding
But still trying to fire the gun – alone.
As I dragged myself up by half-opened
Door of the vehicle, I heard the driver groan.
Gaining consciousness, he explained, "Let's take this gal home!
Let's get out of here!"
The gunner shouted to me, "Can you feed?
"Yes!" I shouted weakly.
"Well, come feed her. Let's take her home!"
Lying flat on my back underneath that Quad-50,
I could see directly up the mountainside.
I was completely exposed to the enemy:
There was no protection from anything falling down that mountainside.
But I never – before – felt more protected: more invincible.
Shooting nearly straight up in the air,

We set that mountainside ablaze
As the driver drove us –
bumpily, bump, bumpily, thump –
out of danger and towards the compound.
The gunner was bleeding but he mechanically pulled the gun's
Butterfly triggers. I was sweating, sore, scraped and scarred.
All four barrels of that Quad-50 were smoking
And they sizzled like red-hot frying pans.

That's what I found myself thinking about.
That's what I was reminiscing about.
What a rush! What a **GREAT** feeling of power!
That's when I came back to myself…
But with a **BIG** grin on my face!
I was smiling!! I was enjoying it!!
Oh, man, what a feeling!!!
Oh, man, what a thrill!!!
I caught myself smiling!!
I shouldn't be enjoying this kind of stuff.
I shouldn't be enjoying these kinds of feelings.
I shouldn't be enjoying these kinds of experiences.
I can't live in this world with these kinds of thoughts
Living inside my head.
So. Well, just maybe….
    Just maybe….
Maybe I should just live in my thoughts.

Roy Lee 'Simon' Jarmon

ANGER SUBDUED

Well, once again, I held the trigger. I'll say that I didn't get angry. As a matter of fact, I acted as if no one was there. As if no one was speaking (hollering) at me. As if no one was behind me honking their horn and cursing in vulgar profanity. Yes, I pretended that they didn't exist or that I didn't hear them.

You see, I was picking up my wife from the hair salon. I drove up to the 'STOP' sign to make a right turn. Before I could continue, I saw her walking toward me, and she got into the car.

"Where's my checkbook?" she said. She had asked me to bring her blue checkbook from her black purse on the bed. I gave her a blue checkbook and turned on the car's emergency flashers.

She sat there in the passenger's seat and wrote the check, and started back to the salon to pay her bill. The car behind me came around and made its turn, and continued on its way. That's the way it should work. However, this other driver pulls up right behind me and starts honking her horn. After 60-plus years, I'm still naive enough to think that she will see my blinkers blinking and she will go around. But, no!!! She just honks louder and faster.

Naturally, I sat there looking ahead and pretending to fumble with the radio. But, of course, I kept glancing in the passenger's rear view mirror. And who is this nut - crossing the intersection from left to right? But not before he approached my window to inform me that this person parked behind me wants me to move my car, as if I can't hear (though that's the way I was pretending).

He's just crossing the street. What does he have to do with this situation? So, you know he got the "STARE". I just looked at him like he had two heads or maybe no head at all. Like "Who are you? And why are you even speaking to me?"

The passenger in the car behind me opened his door and stepped out behind the car. He was yelling something. Exactly what he was saying? I couldn't tell! And I didn't care what he was saying. I was watching his actions. That's what mattered to me.

At that time, I saw my wife - man, isn't she gorgeous? - coming towards the car. I eyed the passenger behind me who was still flailing and waving his arms and yelling and cursing. I wanted to ensure that he didn't approach before my wife was inside and safe. The not-minding-his-business street crosser had faded into the shadows of the night (where he should have always been and not here bothering me.) I opened the car door to assist my wife into the car. She heard the passenger behind us yelling and shouting and cursing. She became excited: afraid. "Let's go! Let's get out of here!" she yelled in excitement.

At this time, cars were passing on my perpendicular street from left to right and from right to left. "Let's go! Let's get out of here!" my wife continued shouting anxiously. "Didn't you hear what he was saying?"

I almost lost my control and was about to yell at her. "I can't go anywhere right now; there's traffic!" But as I inched forward, turning off my emergency flashers and turning on my right-turn signal, I got a break. And as I was making my right turn, I took one last glance into my rear-view mirror and experienced a feeling of satisfaction. A feeling of gladness - a you-take-that kind of feeling - as I took my last look at the flailing, frantic, yelling, cursing guy and lady behind me.

As I sped up toward home, a wry smile came over my face. I realized the smile that arose amidst my approaching headache because of what I had done to the flailing, frantic, yelling, and cursing persons who were behind me. No! No! Not that! Not the reality. But really, what I envisioned (yes, that's probably the best word) could or even would have happened. Just think! Supposed he would have approached my vehicle and I had my weapon cocked, aimed and ready. Yes, that was what I envisioned. Wow! Just imagine. So, who am I? Yes, who am I? For certain, I had provoked him. Intentionally!!!

Roy Lee 'Simon' Jarmon

TO TELL THE TRUTH

Oh, how I laughed
and told some jokes
and shared in the party's fun.
I smoked my smokes
And drank my drinks
And mingled with everyone.
I was pretty smart so
I worked really hard
As a programmer with AT&T.
Then I met my wife
Who was to share my life
And we lived... (happily?)
We had some good times
And made good money
And lived a usual existence.
We maintained high hopes
For our union and our son,
But there was something that had more persistence.
My bright lights grew dim
And my dim lights grew dimmer
And a black cloud hovered over the place.
Every time I would turn around
My smiles would turn to a frown
And tears constantly traveled down my face.
My smoking was a curse
And my drinking got worse
And my control went AWOL on ol' Sarge.
None of my tactics seemed to work
And it made me feel like a jerk
So I said, "Retreat!" instead of "Charge!"

Then I said, "Good-bye!"
To my drinking and smoking
And my violence turned into a 'sweet tooth'.
Eventually, my loud shouts
Turned into half smiles
But the tears still rained - to tell the truth.

Roy Lee 'Simon' Jarmon

IF PEOPLE KNEW

Why, certainly!
I do agree.
I just can't stand
A whimpering man.
If he starts to cry,
I'll say, "Good-bye!"
But for a very, very,
Very good reason,
I may attempt my hand at treason.
And if I get bold,
And then even bolder,
I may allow him to cry
Upon my shoulder.
But he must promise to never tell.
For fear of living his life in HELL!
He must never even hint
To tell the story
That I once stepped out
Of Man's territory.
Not even a hint or a tease
Or we'll both be dead;
And he'll have the grave
Is my only dread.
Surely, there's no need for this
Life-ending fight
If he keeps his head
And his mouth shut tight.
There's no need for anyone to know.
It only happened once
And we were at a show.
There were only a few tears

And I quickly wiped them away.
I didn't even know they were coming
When they appeared that day.
I don't understand how
This happened to me.
It was the strangest thing!
It still seems a mystery.
I was not the least bit sad.
As a matter of fact,
I was extremely glad.
It happened at the circus while we were having fun.
We were hugging each other - me and my son.
And the tears just started dropping
Like it was a rainy day.
I... I... I can't explain it.
I don't know what to say.
Except that it was pleasing-
I felt real good inside:
Which is all the more reason
That it's something to hide.
Shhhh! Quiet! Hush!
Whew! I'd die if someone heard me
Talking about that mush.
Why did it happen to me - a pillar of society?
Why?! Why?! Why?!
Oh, I can just see the headlines, now,
If people knew that I could cry.

Roy Lee 'Simon' Jarmon

Love, Romance
And Such

THESE PICTURES

Spike, I thought you were a friend of mine!
Yes, I really thought you were.
But then you wrote me a letter
And you sent me these pictures of her.

Now, I sit and watch these pictures -
Day after night after day.
And when I try to go to sleep at night
These pictures won't go away.

It's not that I don't want to think about her:
It's just that she's not here.
It's hard being away from such a sweet thing
Who was once my Darling Dear.

She's a lady who's beautiful, cherished, and sweet
With a body so lovely and fine.
I'm a man who's dejected, lonely, and bored
Because she's no longer a lady of mine.

These three pictures are my only joy -
Though I must sit and wonder,
"Why must the lady who brings true happiness
Just be a girl of yonder?"

I know it must be my fault
For not letting my true self shine.
But I'm alone
Now that she's gone,
But I hope and pray
Every day,
That I'll see her one more time!!!

Roy Lee 'Simon' Jarmon

I USED TO DREAM OF QUEENS

I used to dream of Queens.
I used to dream of Goddesses of Love
        And Goddesses of Romance
                And Beauty
    To be by my side.
    To be in my arms -
            Lying beside me
    In my bed.
And I deserned myself to be
A shadow of what I've been
        not knowing exactly who I am.

I no longer dream of Queens
I no longer dream of Goddesses of Love
        Nor Goddesses of Romance
                And Beauty.

My Darling and I sleep arm-in-arm.
She's was by my side -
        Lying beside me
        In my bed.
In you, My Love, I now see
A reflection of what I've been
And who I am.

In my dreams of Queens and Goddesses
        I was a dreamer.
In my dreams of you, my Love,
        I am a King.

Roy Lee 'Simon' Jarmon

NEXT TO YOU

It seems I've made
A terrible mistake
In having a wonderful
Time with you.
Now my heart and soul
Are sad,
And lonesome and blue.

You did and said
So many things
That I wanted
To hear and be;
But, oh, the sadness
I now feel
When you're not
Here with me.

You said I rekindled
Your sexual flame
That you thought you no longer
Possessed.
But it was you
Who rekindled me
And without you
I'm a mess.

Really my whole
Constitution is rejected,
Warped, and wrecked.
I try to console
My heart's desire
By saying,
"Oh, what the heck?!"

"I know that I'm not angry!"
Is what
I keep telling myself.
I know
That I shouldn't be with you -
You belong to
Someone else.

So I must face reality -
That which is
Real and true.
But the only thing
That consoles my heart
Is lying here next to you.

Roy Lee 'Simon' Jarmon

THE MOMENT OF TRUTH

I've had my share
Of pretty faces with empty souls,
Of beautiful bodies with empty hearts,
And of lovely places
Visited
With an enticing dress,
Wrapped around shiftless
    Shady,
Types of girls.

I don't want a pretty face
That doesn't enclose a mind
That projects an intelligence
Worthy of the title,
'WOMAN'.

No more voluptuous bodies
Without a spirited soul
Filled with the love of loving.

Life is too short
To settle for
One hurt after another.

One must realize
That hurts can be
Eternal.

Those restless moments;
Those torturing agonies;

Those horrific, nightmarish
Dreams of another rejection
Can become apparent
If love
Is forgotten.

I found that
My realization of love
Had become apparent
Right before my eyes -
In you.

My recuperative hibernation
Is over.
Nothing can go wrong
Because the moment
Of truth is here.
I know it!
I can feel it!
I can feel it in my bones!
I can feel it in my soul! I...
Can feel it in the air!
It's all around!

But,
When you said,
"No!"
It came to me:
Hell, I felt that way before.

Roy Lee 'Simon' Jarmon

VICATIOUS CONTINUNITY

Every night I look into her eyes:
    And the intoxicating effect
    Causes a dizziness in me.

Everything seems up-side down;
    Turning, whirling,
    Round and round
    As I feel myself drawn
    To her lush,
    Warm mouth.

I kiss her sweet, hot lips
    In the morningtime
    And notice the bruises on her
    Neck that I caused during the night
    In my uncontrollable passions of
    Ecstasy.

During the day, I'm engrossed
    With her voluptuous and sexy body
    That vibrated so arrogantly,
    At first,
    And then slowed to the swaying

Of a hill-side tree-top
    In an almost calm
    Morning's breeze.

In the evenings I return
    To the continuous effervescence
    Of the gaiety of her soul -
    That is still yet unborn.

I'm constantly in the vice
    Of this unique creature,
    Day and night,
    Night and day,
    And I feel that this
    Is where I want to be,

But I know that
    Someday, I must
    Somehow and in
    Someway,
    Rid myself of these dreams,
    Because she's no longer
    Around.

                    Roy Lee 'Simon' Jarmon

THE GIRL NEXT TO ME

"You know I've seen
Every Zodiac sign there is
On that wall
More than once,
With the exception of mine.
Take yours, for instance.
What is your sign?"

That's it! That's what I'll say.
There's no better way
To start a conversation.
Perfect!!
That's it!
That's the way I'll start it.

I knew she was doing it on purpose -
her knee: slightly caressing my thigh.
It was her signal that she
Was ready for conversation. It's time!

And she's beautiful, too.
Such a fine body.
A nice body to dance with.
To Hold it firmly against mine.
    Her soft body;
    Her Warm body -
So warm - I can imagine.

Okay! Okay! Okay!
I've looked pass her long enough.

It's time.
It's time I spoke.
Enough nerves now. Here goes!
What to say, now?
Ah, yes! Here goes!

I, nervously excited, whirled
To see
    her half-emptied glass;
    Her crumpled cigarette butt;
    Her lip-stick smeared napkin,
And, it seemed,
    Her invisible footprints
Leading to the exit –
Joined by another's
Just at the final curtain.

Roy Lee 'Simon' Jarmon

THE QUESTION

How does one erase the words
    That he has once said -
Even when they are words that
    You didn't mean?
How do you change the colors
    From red
When they should have been
    Painted green?
How do you begin again and
    And begin again at the start?
But my burning question is,
    "How do you unbreak my heart?"

Roy Lee 'Simon' Jarmon

LOVE IS IT

I can't get you off my mind.
I think about you all the time:
At work! At church! And when I'm walking the street.
Wherever I go; in every place!
I hear your voice! I see your face!
Even in the lonely crowds of unknown people I meet.

I'm not complaining - bragging really!
Some of you may say I'm acting silly.
And I don't care about that in the least bit.
On my face is a constant smile.
Others notice it and wonders, while
I know what the reason is: LOVE is it.

Roy Lee 'Simon' Jarmon

OF MAE MAE

The gleam in her eyes
shone like the sun's ray
when I asked her
if I could stay
the night with her.
To my surprise,
she said that I may.

Jokingly, I asked,
"Your place or mine?"
I couldn't have guessed that
I was about to find
that she was more woman
than I'd dreamed she'd be.

With an affectionate stare,
she came toward me
and held her warm body
next to mine.
I started kissing her

eagerly, time after time
with heated passion
and uncontrollable desire.
She, willingly and readily,
increased the fire.

She rubbed her fingers
through my hair
and whispered in my ear,
"I love you, Dear!"

my hands reached wildly;
here, there, here,
finding nothing
but hot, soft flesh
that shot a steady flow of
pleasing pain into my fingertips.
The sensation seeped throughout my body
to settle within my swelling heart
and trembling lips.

Burning with the wine of ecstasy,
I rapidly and randomly kissed her face
that glowed with a honey-loved scent.
From her mouth gushed
her flaming tongue
as I gently bent

(in a motion quite serene)
to drink of the heavenly spirits
of her succulent passions, but
the alarm clock disturbed my dream.

Roy Lee 'Simon' Jarmon

VALUE

I was just thinking
    That everything has value,
And,
      If you could acquire
         Everything there is,
Then
         You could be
    The most valuable person in the world.

Being that we are people
         And people
         Are not perfect,
    We can't get everything;
But
    Everything does have value.

Take a driver's license
         (for instance).
To purchase one,
      It cost you
    Just a few dollars.
To be caught

Without it
    Its cost is over
         Many times the price.

Now,
    Think about that.
Compare it to anything.
Compare it to
    A former lover.

Roy Lee 'Simon' Jarmon

JUST BARELY KNOW YOUR NAME

I just barely know your name
But you are always on my mind.
I've talked to you from time to time
And you have set my heart a-flame.

I have visualized US in my head,
While we held each other near
And whispered words we love to hear
As we tumbled in the bed.

You have my heart singing a song.
I just can't wait to get there
And caress your long, beautiful hair
While we make love all night long.

Roy Lee 'Simon' Jarmon

WHETHER THE WEATHER

In the hum drum chatter
          Of the rain -
   Splish, splash,
       Spitter, spatter-
Against my windowpane
        (during my lone lonesome hours),
Over and over I hear your name
   And see your face in the misty showers.

Under the beaming, glaring sun-
            HOT -
   projecting it's sweltering
       (sweating or not
          To walk or run)
            Temp that beat,
              Beat,
              Beat.
I, nonetheless, wipe
        Whether sweat or not
         And run
Though I to sheltering
      To watch your swaying,
Wavy image in the heat.

When the night has lain
It's silent, black shroud
Like the dew
     (as wet as rain)
Upon the land,
     Hark!

I hear my heartbeat
    (uncalmly loud)
And stretch forth my hand
      To you
Waiting silently
    And
Unseen
    In the dark.

Roy Lee 'Simon' Jarmon

NOT WORTH THE GAMBLE

I rolled them once. They came up five.
I rolled again. They came up seven.
Why not two or three, or four or six?
Or eight or nine, or ten or eleven?
Oh, well, it's only money, and
I'll get some more somehow someday.
I probably lost because of fate,
And life's just a gamble anyway.

I got busted at the card table.
Though unhappy I discarded my clothes.
I guess it's just a game of chance
Plus it keeps me on my toes.
I lost my property (land and house),
And that kept me on the roam.
It didn't damage my ego too much;
It was Just a house - not a home.

But then I met this lady sweet:
And I really enjoyed her company.
I've grown very weak for her,
And I want to keep her here with me.
I've had the chance to be with others
Who were just as sweet and just as fine.
But, finally, I've decided that
I've gambled my very last time.

Roy Lee 'Simon' Jarmon

OBSERVATIONS

I've been noticing you these last couple of days.
I've been noticing you in quite a few ways.
I've noticed your eyes are all shady and shifty.
The style of your clothes is rather common but nifty.
That body of yours is so sexy and lean.
Those breasts you have are the fullest I've seen.
Your personality, too, is so friendly and kind:
It alone has made you an admirer of mine.
You're very studious, and you're helpful to many.
For you, I can say that I have affection aplenty.
When I take all of your traits and mold them into one,
You have a beauty more radiant than the sun.
To pass you up, I know, would be a crime;
So take my hand, Darling; let's share our time.

Roy Lee 'Simon' Jarmon

MARGARETTE'S SONG

I thought she was a no-good whore.
Her attitude proved it all the more.
She's no good; not even to herself.
Every man has her picture upon his shelf.
She is a poor excuse for a girl.
None can be cheaper anywhere in the world.
She's probably no good in her books nor class.
I'm ashamed to be seen with that type of lass.
She seems the type that all players want to meet.
She's not as decent as the woman on the street.
She has a nice body, but that's all she's got.
It's easy to see that she stays hot.
She stays at the club and as high as she can be.
I couldn't stand for her to be seen with me.

Then, all of a sudden, the truth came to light.
I happened to walk her to the dorm one night.
I found her the opposite of what I expected.
My thoughts have now been redirected.
My former thoughts had me climbing the wall.
She's really an intelligent person after all.
She's not at all like the ones on the street.
She's very, very beautiful and really kind of sweet.
But there's a fault I hope that she gets rid of.
But it's nothing that can't be cured by love.
She's a much better person than I thought she could be.
And now I am proud that she was seen with me.
I think that no one has her picture on their shelf.
She's just another young lady who's searching for herself.
She's as pleasing as a brand-new moon.
I hope she finds herself and real soon.

Roy Lee 'Simon' Jarmon

IF I COULD WAIT UNTIL ETERNITY

If I could wait until eternity
Then I could wait until forever
      For your love.
    I could wait until
You have drowned all your fears
In a sea of positivity.
    I could wait until you
Have grown a shatter-proof shield
Around your heart.
    I could wait until all your doubts
And disbeliefs are estranged
And dissipated.
    But man's span of life
Is much too short to wait
Until tomorrow
    And I want you now.
I not only want you
For my sake, but
    I want you because
I need you for our sake.
I need you and
I need loving-
Your loving.
      To love is not enough
Without reciprocation.
For being loved,
    Being wanted,
    Being needed
Determines the longevity of my whole,
      My soul,

My being.
I cannot allow my incompleteness
To become more incomplete,
So I must beseech
That you, now
    Make a choice -
Give me your love
Or
Give me back my heart!
    FREE!

Roy Lee 'Simon' Jarmon

LEARN TO SAY GOOD-BYE

When I was a small boy, I saw on TV
A very touching story that's still with me.
While watching the story, I began to cry.
The story was called "Learn To Say Good-bye".

I've told this story from time to time
To ease the pain in friends of mine.
I've used the expression when people ask, "Why?"
I say, "Everyone must learn to say good-bye".

We'll all have heartaches as sure as we're born.
We'll all someday need a shoulder to lean on.
So, I've used that expression sometimes as a crutch
When a person has lost someone they love so much.

Now I must say it somehow, someday.
Someone has left me. She was taken away.
But will I get through it? I will, I pray.
But now, I'd like to see her come back to stay.

Roy Lee 'Simon' Jarmon

MY ONLY ONE

I tell myself I love you,
And I do;
But how much? But why?
Because you're here.
Because you say you'll stay.
It makes me grateful
That you feel that way,
And I believe
That maybe you do, too
Or
At least you want to.

I tell you of my sorrows,
My sadness, my blues:
And your shoulder and ears are there.
I tell of my hopeful tomorrows,
Today's expensive dues,
And why I'm not getting anywhere.

I look at other women -
So fine, so loving, so fair-
Shaking their backs, bouncing their uppers
And flinging their pretty hair.
I dance with them, the thingamajig.
I play the waiter or kiss and run.
I give them laughter, and that's all y'all
'Cause you're my only one.

Roy Lee 'Simon' Jarmon

I COULD HAVE JUST CLOSED MY EYES

I could have just closed my eyes -
Never to see again -
When I learned that you were leaving:
Moving far away.
There is no beauty if there is no sight
And I would have wished not to see
Had it not been for my burning desire
To see your glowing, wonderful smile.

If my arms and legs had fallen off,
They would not have been missed
Because there's no place I'd choose to walk
If the path didn't lead to you.
Being armless would not be a handicap
If you are not around to hold.

I could have just closed my mouth –
Never to speak another word,
Never to eat another bite-
Because there's no reason for nourishment
When you are not here with me.
Never to speak would have been my wish
Had it not been for my desperate need
To tell you how much I love you.

Roy Lee 'Simon' Jarmon

BEING IN LOVE

Darling,
    I love you,
But
    There's one thing-
I think I love you too much.

I don't ever believe that
    I can love you
        Too much,
It's the depth-
    I love you
        Too deeply.

I even hope to love you
    Much deeper than now –
        It's only that
            I'm afraid.

I'm not scared to say that
    I'm not afraid
        Of love,
    And I'm certainly not
Afraid
        Of you.

It's hurt that I fear.
    I hate to imagine
        Being hurt again,
But I love you
    So much

That
      I hope it's just
            My imagination.

Darling,
      Will you love me
            Forever?

Roy Lee 'Simon' Jarmon

AS LONG

I don't have money,
    Fortune or fame.
I wouldn't even know how
    To play the game
    If I had the money to.

But I'm not worried
    Nor forlorn
Because I don't need it
    As long-
    As long as I have you.

Roy Lee 'Simon' Jarmon

BENEATH THE OLD OAK

The tall, slender, scarcely planted pines
Stood lifeless on the hillside
But made the air heavy and dense
With the quiet smell of their souls.

As I brooded beneath
The large, drooped, aged, lone oak
That stood so proudly there,
I thought of her and whispered to myself,
"I love you! I love you!"

Then when the bobbing of her head
Darted upon the face of the moon,
Immediately I ran - in a flash –
Towards her while the white moonlight And gray shadows played
Psychedelic patterns upon my casual wear.

I streaked towards her with
Superhuman speed while the wind tore
Around the edges of my glasses and
Snatched from my eyes the tears of joy.

As the thoughts of my reasons for living
Raced ahead of me,
I heard the thunderous shouting of my heart saying,
"I love you so dearly and so deeply!"

While the distance between us slowly decreased,
The tail of her gown waved at her back
As if some desperate, almost weightless
Creature, held a firm hand at its hem.

I whirled her dizzily in a circle
When my arms were securely around her waist
While she tightly held my neck and
Eagerly kissed me randomly about my face
With her hot, moist mouth.
I gushed in a deep-throated groan,
"I love you, my Darling!"

Slowly we strolled hand in hand,
Heads up high, from the separate but same
Emotions of frantic love.

We gently rolled among the lightly-damp coolness
Of the dew and the unseeing eyes of the light shadows.
I could hear the still noises:
    (the loud silence of romantic squeals;
    the light darkness of feminine gasps,
    And the brightness of a throated moan) -
"I love you! I love you! I love you!"

Oh, the smile that old oak tree must have made
As I held it tightly in my arms and squeezed it
While she gaily skipped and ran up the hill.

At the top she turned and waved and threw a BIG kiss.
I waved joyously and hollered at the top of my lungs,
"I love you......................................."
(Not knowing that this would be
The last time that I'd see her).

Roy Lee 'Simon' Jarmon

ONE HELL OF A WOMAN

Some may say that she's no good:
That she's rotten to the core.
But I see a lot of beauty in her.
She's One Hell Of A Woman.

Of course, she's made mistakes.
Everyone makes one or more.
I think her mistakes really brought her out.
They made her One Hell Of A Woman.

She, in aging, has become refined,
But that's no reason to get sore.
She's quite young, yet, with plenty of life.
Yes, she's One Hell Of A Woman.

Whenever someone is treated unfairly,
It sometimes brings me to tears.
She's her own woman, and I like her for it.
Yes, One Hell Of A Woman she is.

Roy Lee 'Simon' Jarmon

LOVE PAINS

Throughout my travels in life -
in hopes of finding
the perfect wife -
I've met girls of many types.

But I find it very strange
that they tend to arrange
their excuses in the same
manner,
"You always hurt the one you Love."

From my experience and understanding
of the things that Love's demanding,
I must disagree with all the rest;
even though it's quoted
by some of the best.

I don't think it's true at all
that you hurt the one you Love,
but instead, the one that Loves you.

In this respect, I must say
(for the hurt that I caused today),
it would seem that I don't care.
But I don't want you feeling like that:
thinking I'm ready to get my hat.

I said that I'd never fall in Love again.
I actually thought I wouldn't.
I really believed that I couldn't
until you came along
and made my life a happy song.

The sparkle in your eyes
seemed to reach out and touch my heart
like the sun's rays
glittering through the colors of a rainbow
after a spring or summer sprinkle.

Then there's that golden glow of your face
that oozes slowly
From its secret place.
And those sweet expressions
that tickle my very being.
All my dreary thoughts and feelings
become misty and seem to evaporate-
like water from a steaming pot
on a wildly roaring fireplace –
when I pull you gently close to me
and feel the lint-like softness
of your bosom
pressed firmly against my chest.

Ohhhh! The silky smoothness of your skin
feels like satin sheets
caressing my nude body
as I slowly glide among its warmness.

Your presence is like
an enchanting fog of yellowish-gold moonbeams
flowing evenly throughout.
It causes a slight dizziness in me
that calms and quiets my soul
as I weakly succumb
and lie peacefully in eternity.

Yes, this is Love!
This is the Love I seek: so calm,
so gentle,
so meek.

I apologize,
so forgive me,
if you can.
I Love you.
I'll never hurt you
again.

Roy Lee 'Simon' Jarmon

SOMETHING IN MY EYES

Because of you
There is something in my eyes.
I can't wipe it out
Nor rub it out.
Sometimes it causes a lazy tear
To creep downwardly on my cheek.

It's even reached my heart.
Sometimes it sputters
And flutters. Sometimes
It pounds -
        My heart does -
And sometimes it skips a beat.

I'm also convinced
That it has reached my legs too.
As frail and weak
As they really are,
They sometimes feel strong-
        So strong -
And are willing to run miles
        And miles
And miles...

It's your gracious acceptance
That's in my eyes.
It's your aurora of sweetness
That's gently crushing my heart.
And it's your soft and warm body
That makes me want to run-
        To you.

Roy Lee 'Simon' Jarmon

QUIET FIRE

I'm trying to decipher this change
That's resurfacing from inside.
It's like an over-laughed situation
Where you feel you've happily cried.

Sometimes it makes me feel good-
Really I should say 'GREAT'!
And time is no bother - as if still –
Be it early or be it late.

This happiness is tugging inside of me,
Pushing out the invisible truth;
And laying heavily upon my chest
Those golden thoughts of youth.

This movement churns inside of me
Secreting out passion and desire.
And all that matters to me is
This voluptuous lady - my *QUIET FIRE*!

Roy Lee 'Simon' Jarmon

MY SWEET, INNOCENT ONE

Oh, my sweet, innocent one
My heart is sinking for you.
I find you a likely lovable girl
Whose love can be so true.
I try to avoid making the mistake
Of being a lonely man.
So what else is there left to do
But to fall in love again?
Every time I fell in love before,
She broke the heart of this poor man.
But you're so beautiful and so fine
That I'll chance getting it broken again.

Roy Lee 'Simon' Jarmon

MARY

<u>M</u>ay your gracious kindness
<u>A</u>lways shine bright and
<u>R</u>adiant and alive;
<u>Y</u>es, like smoldering embers
    burning within my Heart.

Roy Lee 'Simon' Jarmon

UPS AND DOWNS, INS AND OUTS

Whenever I want some colorful loving, I'm dyed up.
I try my sweetness and really get dear(ed) down.
When I tell you of your blindness, I'm eyed up.
I stick out my chest with ego and you act feared down.
Trying to scarf some affection, I get cloaked in.
Trying to inject a little wit, I get joked in.
I try and jail your lies and they get bailed out.
Never are you there when my arms are held out.

You have ice in your heart every time I'm fired up.
And when I mention the truth, I'm lied up.
I tell you of shameful things and I'm jeered down.
I gun up my motor and you really get geared down.
Trying to stir up your sexiness, I get poked in.
I try soft caresses hoping you get gelled out.
Trying to dry up your tears really get me soaked in.
Before I can train anything, I get railed out.

And to say your loudness embarrasses, I get quieted up.
And to mention someone your equal, gosh I get peered down.
And when I say you are too loose, all my hands are tied up.
I tell you of your freakishness, and I'm the one that's weird down.
I tell you we are moving apart and I get neared in.
But act like I'm getting rough and I get tear(ed) in.
I try and float into your heart and I get sailed out.
And when I try and head up your passions, I get tailed out.

And mention how you string me along, I'm wired up.
But, Baby, you can hang it up now because I'm rye(d) up.
I try and bring my feelings forward and I get reared down.

Yes, I'm going to win this time because I'm beer(ed) down.
Trying not to work you hard, I get yoked in.
I try and speak of oneness and get yelled out.
Watch out! Here I come and I'm smoked in.
Yes, I'm going to fix you now that I'm all ale(d) out.

Roy Lee 'Simon' Jarmon

MARTHA

What kind of name is Martha?
From where do you think it came?
Its derivative means lady:
In Italian and Spanish - the same.

What could you do with a name like Martha?
Well, really, there's no telling.
You could call it, think it, or change it –
And it's pretty alright for yelling.

Artistically picturing a name like Martha
Is a portrait somewhat shady.
The name Martha means nothing to me.
My interest is in the lady.

Placing that name with one such lady
Just makes my heart uncurl.
I don't give a darn about the name 'Martha',
But, oh, how I love that girl!

Roy Lee 'Simon' Jarmon

REBECCA

Remembering good times is
Easy as breathing
Because out-stretched arms
Eagerly beckoned me
Calling. I must say that
Calmness was my least virtue,
Acknowledging her welcoming **LOVE**.

Roy Lee 'Simon' Jarmon

THE OLD HOUSE

by

Roy Lee 'Simon' Jarmon

He had really become attached to that old house. He only liked it, maybe, because it had housed him when there was no other one available. He never expected to stay there. If you had asked him how long he'd be there, when he first moved in, he would've said, "Oh, a couple of days maybe. It's just a temporary stop-over for a while". No, he never intended to stay from the start.

He knew that the old house was a pushover. At first, she wouldn't open her door for him, but he knew that she was no match for his smooth persistence. He moved in, looked around, examined things, and then made himself at home.

Upon his entrance, the old house creaked and shuddered, but with a sigh of relief. Gradually, they became comfortable with each other. The house had a bad place in its ceiling. Her foundation was somewhat weakly constructed because of the many, long years of misuse followed by an era of neglect. Now that the breath of life existed within her, the boards seemed to become revitalized and, seemingly, willing to offer all the shelter she could provide while he lay there and accepted all of it.

Day and night, she would house him and his belongings. When he was gone, she protected his clothes from the naked truth and her heart from the kindling of others. Sometimes it took all that she could stand, but it was worth the effort - a reason to continue existing.

Then, one night when he didn't come home, she shook as if in the midst of a gale or a tremendous storm. It happened again and again and again. He had spent nights in better houses, mobile homes, brick houses and bars, cafes, and cars, and everywhere else - as a matter of fact.

Many months (the house aged as if they were years) passed since that beautiful spring day when he first arrived. Colder weather began to set in. Finally, he returned, made a huge fire in the fireplace, warmed him- self and the house thoroughly, rested for a while, and left again. During his absence, when the fire was about to burn out, a sudden shudder of the house would loosen a board from her body to land close enough to rekindle the dying sparks. Strange as it seemed - it was on her own accord to keep the fire burning for him.

In the meanwhile, his feet crushed the carpet of one place then another until he was no longer welcomed anywhere. He thought, "There is one place left to go – the old house." He then started on his way - again, as nonchalant as ever - not knowing that all he would find was her dusty, cold ashes scattered by the wind from her empty bed where he once lay.

THE END

HAVE YOU EVER SEEN

"Have you ever seen the sun
Shine at night?
Hey, I'm talking
        To you,
            Man!
Do you know anyone
Who can make the sun shine
                At night?
Well, my Beloved can."

Roy Lee 'Simon' Jarmon

I CAN'T SAY, "NO"

I know that I can change my style
    When things start seeming gray.
I know that I can play along to
    Get things going my way.
I know that I can change expressions
    When I want one to turn me loose.
I know that I can string you along
    though I know there is no use.
I know that I can capture attention
    When I am feeling blue,
But there's one thing that I can't do
    And that's saying, "NO" to you.

Roy Lee 'Simon' Jarmon

STUCK

In kindergarten, I got my glue
All over my clothes and hands.
Oh, how my paper clung to me.
I got stuck. I didn't like it.

While aiding in the design of a sheer
And a beautiful evening gown, I grabbed
The garment's hem - filled with pins.
I got stuck. I didn't like it.

I was reared among roses - now my
Favorite flower. Oh, what fragrance!
Oh, what beauty! The rose has. I picked one.
I got stuck. I didn't like it.

I met a joyous and wonderful young lady
And have grown to love her dearly.
When I think of my Darling Dear, I think of LOVE.
I am stuck. And I LOVE it!

Roy Lee 'Simon' Jarmon

Roy Lee "Simon" Jarmon

I WAS ABOUT TO SAY, "I LOVE YOU"

I was about to say, "I love you!"
Before we separated that night.
Surely I would have said it
If we would not have had that fight.
It takes a little while for me to say it;
But when I do, there must be smiles.
My heart was drawing me closer to her,
But she preferred a distance of miles.

Roy Lee 'Simon' Jarmon

ODE TO MY DREAM OF TETRA-VILLE

I was driving down the highway.
    I was driving somewhat slow.
I was chewing gum and drinking beer
    And listening to the radio.

Then something happened under the hood.
    Something exploded - I think.
The car stopped. I gathered my nerves,
    Lit a cigarette, and took a drink.

The ground was poured black with night
    As I sat there all alone.
I could see nothing ahead of me.
    My lights were out - gone.

Then, to my left, there was a light
    Burning dimly across the field.
As I left the car, the wind knifed me –
    Stabbing as if to kill.

I shuddered and shook off some of the chill
    And started towards the house.
Besides the cracklings under my feet,
    Everything was quiet as a mouse.

I slowly neared this old shack
    With its greasy window panes,
And tapped lightly on the shabby door
    Of this ancient, run-down frame.

The dim light beamed through the cracks,
    Upon the ground and onto my face.
I tried to imagine the landlord of this
    Old, dilapidated place.

Soon, I knocked again, harder.
    The door opened with a creak.
I was cautious and maybe scared, but
    The wind said, "Take a peek!"

The room was small (not large at all).
    I'd say fifteen by fifteen.
At the window hung a thin, dusty curtain
    Whose color was formerly green.

There was a small three-legged table,
    Pushed flush against the wall.
There sat an old man a century or more,
    Leaning - about to fall.

I reached to give the old man a hand
    And felt a stare tear into me.
I turned as she thundered the words,
    "Stranger, let him be!".

She was... well, ... sort of fattish
    In a strange, sort of puffy manner.
She stood with her fists tightly clenched
    And her head in a red bandana.

I heard a cough from the old man –
    His eyes were already closed.
His forehead and face were greasy from sweat,
    And something dripped from his mouth and nose.

I shouted, "Wipe the sweat from his face!
    Why don't you help the poor, sick man?"
"He's not sick, my son", she said.
    "I see you don't understand".

"It's my turn next", were the words I heard.
    They came from my right.
I looked and there sat another old man.
    He was sitting just out of the light.

"So, it's your turn next, huh?", I asked.
    "Hey, what's going on here?".
"I'll be glad to explain", the old man said
    As he beckoned me to come near.

"We expected you to arrive before now –
    About three days ago I'd say.
What happened that made you arrive so late?
    Had trouble along the way?".

I was stunned at the old man's words –
    Shocked right out of my mind.
"Just have a seat, and don't you worry!
    Everything's going to be just fine!".

I tried to think of what he meant
    By "what took you so long".
I knew that I wasn't dreaming.
    Something must be wrong.

My mouth was dry as a powder house,
    And I felt I was under a spell.
"I haven't died, have I?", I thought.
    Could I be in Hell?".

"What's the matter with that old man",
    I asked, removing my hat?
"That lady said I didn't understand.
    What did she mean by that?"

The old man at the table by the door
Was emanating a scent that stunk.
I inquired, "Is he an alcoholic?
    What's wrong? Is he drunk?"

His beady eyes tore me apart
    As he slowly shook his head.
"He's not the least bit drunk, my son.
    By now, I'd say he's dead!"

"He was strong, though. Three days dying",
    He said, finishing his beer.
"He promised us that he wouldn't die –
    Not until you got here!"

It's hard to imagine how I looked sitting there
    With my mouth opened wide.
I couldn't restrain the boiling tears,
    Now, settling in my eyes.

I had a-many questions to ask,
    But I didn't know where to start.
I was sweating myself, by now,
    And a throbbing was in my heart.

They were removing that lifeless form
    While I sat there - very still.
I felt as if I was entranced -
    No thoughts, no mind, no will.

The room was floating - dazed and dim.
    Timeless - forever - it whirled.
Then, finally, the two returned,
    But this time with a girl.

Girl is not the name for her!
    Maybe Venus or Goddess or Queen!
Her breasts pulsated with every breath
    And her legs were long and lean.

She had long, black, silky hair
    With small curls at the tips.
A light was sparkling in her eyes,
    And she had the sexiest lips.

She had a small, round chin
    And the smoothest golden cheeks.
She had a cute little funny nose,
    But with beauty that every man seeks.

Her neck was skinny, long and brown.
    My spit had the taste of dirt.
Every time she breathed, it seemed
    That the buttons would fly from her shirt.

She wore old, faded, patched blue jeans
    That hugged, tightly, her wasp-like waist.
They showed her body's perfect imprint -
Every curve, every groove, every space.

My arms slowly, automatically opened,
    Telling her to come to me.
It was like a meeting of the minds
    When she glided upon my knee.

I felt the heat from her buttocks
    And her soft, curvaceous hips.
I felt her nipples against my chest
    As we came lips to lips.

Her tongue was hot as a blaze of fire
    As it darted down my throat.
Her arms had the strength of passionate desire
    As she squeezed me until I choked.

She withdrew her tongue and I saw in one eye
    A tear lying lazily there.
I pulled her head onto my shoulder
    And caressed her coal-black hair.

Then I saw those two still standing there.
    They seemed really full of cheer.
He said, "I almost believed you
    Saying you didn't know why you were here".

The puzzle started to come together
Slowly, piece by piece.
"We're going to leave you two alone.
    Go on! Get the old man a niece!"

That's not the way I get my girls –
    Drawn to her by a spell,
But I couldn't resist that beauty
    Of this... Heavenly Hell.

We made frantic love together.
    She was as passionate as she could be.
I barely had strength to roll off her
    When she climbed on top of me.

That went on in that town of Tetra-ville
    About four months or so.
Then I learned that the old man had died
    Just about a month ago.

"His death's a sure sign that I'm pregnant.
    We're going to have a child!"
She jumped up and shouted and screamed
    As if she was going wild.

After six more weeks of making love
    Until we both were black and blue.
Dream brought me the news one evening –
    The lady had died too.

"Now, there's just the two of us
    And we can make love night and day.
We might as well until the twins arrive"
    Were the words I heard her say.

"Come! Leave! Go with me.
    I'll take you away from here!"
"They told me over and over that
    I should never leave, my Dear."

"But there's a whole, big world out there –
    As wide as it can be!"
"I'm afraid there's no other world.
    Well, not for me!"

"Give me one good reason why."
    "I was told not to by my Pa.
He said that I could never leave.
    He said that it's the law."

We argued more about leaving there
    While her stomach increased in size,
And four days were left she said
    Before the twins would open their eyes.

I told her about hospitals and that
    Children should be born there.
I told her I knew nothing about babies
And no one else is around to care.

Then something made her change her mind.
    What? I don't know!
But she said that I should try to leave
    And that she wanted to go.

For the next two days I worked on the car,
    Trying to fix the trouble.
Somehow I started it to running
    And we left there on the double.

Faster and faster I sped along
    With my eyes straight down the road.
Suddenly my Dream spoke in a foreign tongue,
    And I couldn't break the code.

Some kind of smoke whirled from her body,
    Here face, and hands and feet.
In no time at all a handful of dust
    Was all that was left on the seat.

I tried to think of what was happening.
    What had gone wrong?
I went back to where we had started,
    But... Tetra-ville was gone.

I gathered up that powdery residue
And kissed that tasteless dust.
I thought of the times we had together –
    The smiles, the joys, the lust.

It seems that every time I love,
    My heart ends up in a crash.
What am I doing wrong that make all my lovers
    End up being trash?

Roy Lee 'Simon' Jarmon